M000308709

Crescendo Publishing Presents

Instant Insights on...

BUSINESS

Organizing Your Workspace for a Productivity Boost

Marcia Ramsland

small guides. BIG IMPACT.

Instant Insights On...

Organizing Your Workspace for a Productivity Boost
By Marcia Ramsland

ISBN: 978-1-944177-29-4 (p)
ISBN: 978-1-944177-30-0 (e)

Crescendo Publishing, LLC
300 Carlsbad Village Drive
Ste. 108A, #443
Carlsbad, California 92008-2999

www.CrescendoPublishing.com
GetPublished@CrescendoPublishing.com

What You'll Learn in this Book

Did you know that personal organization is the foundation for improving all productivity and success? A streamlined workspace plus top-notch computer organization will dramatically boost your skills and credibility with Marcia Ramsland's innovative approach as a Business Productivity Expert. You'll learn how to setup a well-organized workplace, best structure your time blocks, pare down your email, and organize your computer documents. Marcia has organized hundreds of clients with these proven principles which will now guide **you** with a step-by-step plan how to double your productivity and maximize your effectiveness whether in a corporate suite, cubicle space, or home office. It will be easier than you think with key strategic changes.

With step-by-step instructions you'll be able to ...

- reduce paper piles around you
- retrieve computer files quickly
- pare down your e-mail
- upgrade your online presence

You'll be motivated to ...

- maintain an organized life

- boost your productivity
- earn a reputation for getting things done
- increase your bottom line
- improve your satisfaction each day

Remember, personal organization is the foundation for all increased productivity and success!

Stepping into an efficient workspace each morning and closing down your well-organized computer at the end of the day will create the relief and personal satisfaction you've been longing for in work and life.

In this book, you'll get **Instant Insights** on...

- Love Your Space, Love Your Work
- Streamline Your Workspace
- Detail and Dismiss Paper Piles
- Catch Up on the Backlog
- Organize Your Computer Files for Fast Retrieval
- Handle Your E-mail More Efficiently
- Spruce Up Your Online Presence
- Create a Dependable Planning Hub
- Work Smarter for a Productivity Edge

A Gift from the Author

I believe in you and want to encourage your success so I am offering generous additional resources to help you implement all the practical ideas in this book including:

- An Office "Before and After" Photo Gallery
- An Additional Article "Create an Inspiring Work Environment"
- A Short Webinar on "5 Keys to Organize Your Time & Your Life!"
- A BONUS 1-on-1 Strategy Call for a "Productivity Boost"

You can access these complimentary bonus materials at:
www.organizingpro.com/bookbonuses

Table of Contents

Dedication

This book is dedicated ...

To My In-Person Clients
who allowed me to enter their space and
organize their business and life systems over the
past thirty years,

To My Virtual Clients
who currently coach with me to achieve the
same results in a shorter amount of time from
anywhere in the world,

To You, My Busy New Friend
who has a thirst for practical steps for more time
and less stress at work

Your workspace is the hub for all you do. Make
every day more productive by intentionally
incorporating these steps to achieve great
success in work and life. I know you can do it!

Cheering you onward,

Marcia Ramsland,
The Business Productivity Coach
www.organizingpro.com
"Coaching Busy People to Make Every Day Count!"

Love Your Space, Love Your Work

The faster the pace of your life, the more organized you need to be!

YOU are a very important person to all the people around you, whether online, offline, or in person.

Your business, your boss, your customers, and your family depend on you to do well.

Yet how many times do you finish the day feeling less than successful with what you've accomplished? Do you feel defeated because all your good intentions didn't happen? As I tell all my clients (and now I'm telling you), a day's less-than-stellar results are not a personal character flaw. It just means your systems are broken and are letting you down. They need to be fixed, and we can do that together!

Doing Well in Business and Life Depends on 3 Things

Doing well in work and life depends on three foundational setups for your success.

1) Your Organized Workspace

Does your workspace support you like a well-oiled machine with everything organized and at your fingertips? Your organized workspace is the foundation for doing your best work every day.

2) Your Organized Digital World

Are your computer files organized, your in-box pared down, and your social media showing up with just the right timing and voice? Fast retrieval and brief but timely personal interactions are the name of the game these days.

3) Your Maximized Productivity Systems

Are your habits and planning systems dependable for the best YOU showing up to work each day for maximum productivity? Your planning and output can be multiplied when you know how to identify and fix what needs to be improved. This is what puts you in the driver's seat of your life again.

My Promise to You: An organized workspace and digital world (computer, e-mail, social media) will boost your productivity, earn you a reputation for getting things done, increase your bottom line, and improve your satisfaction each day.

Once we organize your workspace, including your computer and online world, you will actually begin to love your work again. You can advance to a new job or career or increase your profits as a business owner. As an executive, you can set the pace for heightened productivity for everyone in your company. When you change, the people around you change and generally for the better. Be the leader they follow.

Do My Systems Really Matter All That Much?

One large organization called me in as a consultant to figure out why their clientele felt they were being ignored. In three key training sessions and twenty-minute personal consults with each of the 150 staff members, I coached every person in an intensive five-week period. By reviewing each person's paper and e-mail setup, the solution became clear.

The problem? Too much clutter in everyone's e-mail in-box. Higher-level management had fewer than forty e-mails in their in-box, and the average staffer had 400 "to not forget" anything. The result? If each of the 150 workers left only ten e-mails a day unanswered, that would mean 1,500 people per day were being ignored, and complaints were mounting.

The solution? Everyone streamlined their personal setup, eliminated distracting clutter, and trimmed down their e-mail in-box. The organization doubled in size and is thriving today.

Business Growth Begins with Personal Productivity

In top-notch organizations, customer care begins with individual productivity. It comes down to setting yourself up for personal success each and every day. Establish solid foundations of personal organization, and you will see your time multiplied in your daily work.

Over the past three decades I have organized hundreds of clients and thousands of audience participants. The systems I have developed include proven step-by-step directions to fine-tune your workspace. Everyone who follows them finds the same result—immediate relief as they finish one section at a time. You can acquire these same skills ... and the same results, too!

My goal in this book is to share with you exactly how you can live what I call the "Easy, Simple, and Productive" lifestyle at work. It can be done. By organizing your workspace and your digital world on all your screens, your productivity will immediately improve. You'll accomplish more in less time and step away from your work each day with a greater sense of accomplishment.

This is your time! You can get organized, and I'll be your coach to get you there. Let's begin.

Your Instant Insights...

- Personal organization helps you accomplish tasks faster, which always gives you more time and control.

- Any disorganization causes you to avoid issues and results in bigger problems down the road.

- Stay organized by setting up systems that become dependable daily habits.

Start with Your Desktop

Think of your desktop as a runway for takeoff each morning. Clear the clutter the day before for a smooth beginning.

Organizing your workspace will be like having a fresh start at work—a new beginning. Your work life will become easier once you've established a place and a space for everything. You'll actually look forward to going to work each day once everything is cleaned up and put away.

In my experience with hundreds of clients across the country, this initial three-step desk organizing plan is all you need to get the momentum—and relief—started for setting up your workspace for more productivity. Get ready. Here we go!

Begin Simply with Two "Before" Pictures

Begin right now by stepping back and snapping two photos with your cell phone. Take one of your workspace, including the surrounding wall space and floor. This gives you the big picture of your workspace.

Then step in closer and take another photo of just your desktop and the wall space above it. This shows you exactly what you are stepping into each day to produce your best. It's a real eye-opener, and it might not be pretty!

Now look at your two pictures, and you'll see the real condition of your workspace. Do you see the piles of paper, Post-it notes, and wall items that should be cleared up? Likely you'll see things you never noticed before.

The reason we don't see these things in our surroundings is our mind cleverly tricks us with "visual tune out." Just like papers on our refrigerator that we ignore every time we go to pull out the milk, we don't see them. We mentally ignore them.

At work, "visual tune out" means that when we dive into work each morning, our mind tunes out the papers and clutter around us. But as the day goes on, we experience more mental fatigue and wonder why we can't focus in the afternoon. Our subconscious is distracted, fighting to ignore the clutter around us as we try to focus on the tasks at hand. That's a mental drain right off the bat we are going to fix!

Do a Quick 3-Step Desk Cleanup

Is there a way to easily change that? Of course. Simply stand up right now, and spend the next few minutes following these three steps.

Step #1 – Neatly Stack Desktop Papers on One Side of Your Desk

Stand and do this step in ten minutes or less. Just quickly stack papers on one side of your desk in a neat pile. Don't get bogged down in what needs to be done. We'll get to that shortly.

As you do this, however, you can paper-clip papers that you spot that belong together. File things immediately when you know where they go. Eliminate sticky notes in your workspace.

This is a very short desktop cleanup that should finish with a neat stack of papers on one side and a clear workspace in the center of the desk.

Step #2 – Do Some Housekeeping

Now completely dust and clean your whole desktop. This simple act will help you feel better just by corralling paper clips, business cards, and hidden pens.

Then empty the wastebasket and recycle bins. Empty wastebaskets are one sign of an organized office. This attention to detail ensures you will get rid of clutter faster as you work.

Also, look under your desk, return items that belong elsewhere, and take home personal items. One New York City client found fifteen pairs of dress shoes under her desk for her winter commute in boots. She took the majority of them home and still dressed well with fewer of them she carefully selected for client meetings.

Step #3 – Stage the Top of Your Desk

Lastly, stage the top of your desk. Designate the very best locations for optimal efficiency for your landline, cell phone, computer, and current paperwork.

- Phone: Keep your cell phone in one place on your desk, and if you have a landline, position it so that you pick it up with your non-writing hand to take notes as you talk.

- Computer: Place your computer and monitors in front of you, and keep cord clutter out of sight. Maintain a clear workspace in front of the monitor(s) so that you can easily type, but never over paperwork.

- Current Paperwork: Designate one side of your desk for paperwork you are working on. Usually the side that you enter to sit at your desk is best or against a wall.

Finishing Up

Now stand back and take two "After" photos from the exact same view where you started. Wow! Celebrate your improvements, and enjoy your new space now that you have a visually clear workspace. You'll feel better working here, and you'll be ready for the next step.

Your Instant Insights...

- Organizing your desktop is the quickest way to clear your mind and get focused.

- Invest the time to get your desk organized, and you'll reap the rewards immediately. Less on your desk is always better.

- Stay organized by practicing my famous "2-Minute Pickup": spend two minutes putting things away whenever you leave your workspace or change projects.

Replace "The Paper Pile" with a Master List

One pile sitting out is the beginning of a complicated life. Put the pile away, paper by paper, and leave a master list in its place.

Now that you've cleared your desk, you are ready to go through the neat stack of papers left sitting on the side of your desktop. This may be what you've been avoiding, but if you follow these steps, you will get through it today!

I call this neat stack of papers "The Pile" because of its continual presence and importance to current work. You'll soon replace it with a master list of the tasks it represents.

Before you do that though, you need to streamline your supplies to make the process go faster. You'll waste time if you are wading through a cluttered supply drawer looking for a working pen or the right size paper clips.

The Bull's-Eye Principle

To streamline your supplies, think of a target with circles around it. Sitting in your desk chair, you are the center of the bull's-eye. Everything around you is the ever-widening circle of supplies you reach for to do your work.

The Inner Bull's-Eye Circle: Supplies you use daily that are within the sweep of your arm in a small desk drawer or a shelf above your desk

The Middle Bull's-Eye Circle: Supplies you use weekly and stand or stretch for, such as a three-hole punch or your computer bag

The Outer Bull's-Eye Circle: Supplies you use monthly and that you need to walk to retrieve them, like archived files or new manila folders

Streamline Your Supplies

Open your desk drawer, empty the contents onto the clear center of your desk, and wipe out the drawer. Now put back the supply divider tray (or get one if you don't have one), and include only the supplies you currently use.

The basic supplies you need for an efficient office are the following: (1) large and small paper clips,

(2) rubber bands,
(3) sticky notes,
(4) tape, (5) ruler,
(6) scissors,
(7) letter opener, and (8) pens and markers.

Excess pens, markers, and unused supplies take up space and slow you down. Be ruthless about getting rid of them. Donate excess supplies to a school or charity. Take home important personal items that clutter your drawer. One drawer is generally enough. Keep your supplies lean and clean for speed as you work. Simplify!

Why Is a Paper Pile a Problem?

A paper pile represents one or more of the following:

- Current work that needs to be done
- Project work you didn't integrate into your schedule
- Stray papers you just didn't know what to do with

All three are distractions that will keep you from focusing and producing your best work.

Start Organizing "The Pile"

To begin organizing the paper pile, follow these three steps. You will cut your time in half if you do it standing. The steps for the quickest paper-pile sort are the following:

1) Turn "The Pile" Upside Down and Go Through It Paper by Paper

Why upside down? Because the oldest papers are on the bottom, and the older they are, the easier they are to deal with so don't be intimidated. You can handle it. It's only paper. List, file, or recycle each paper until the ever-present pile is gone.

2) List Actionable Items on a To-Do List

You can list "to-do's" on a single pad of paper or a digital task list or file that needs to be done before you put it away.

As my organizing expert friend, Julie Morgenstern, says, "You are more likely to take action on an item on a to-do list, than a task lost in a stack of papers." So true!

3) Put Away All Papers in the Pile—One by One!

The goal is to put all the papers away in files or put their information away digitally. Only the master list of To-Dos is left in its place. The most used paper-filing categories you can use to put your papers away include these:

* Client Files. This is easiest to file because they have a home by client name. Client files are important, and if they look dog-eared, make a note of that as a To-Do on your master list. Make new labeled client files later this week.

* Project Files. Project files are topics that you are currently working on and must have eight sheets of paper to warrant their own hanging folder. Create a file if you don't have one, especially for reoccurring papers on the same topic.

* To-Do File. Put single sheets of paper in a single "To-Do" file, **ONLY** after the task is written on your master to-do list. Do not file without writing it on a visible list you keep on your desk!

* Temporary File. Place brochures, flyers, and advertising you are not sure if you will act on in a file labeled "Temporary." Clean it out the last day of the month. This will keep lower-priority papers from becoming mixed in with your important work. If you need it before the end of the month, you'll retrieve it before then. If not, on the last day of the month, you will quickly know whether to keep it or recycle it.

* Recycle and Shred Files. Once you have purged your office paperwork, you can replace a bulky recycle bin with a "Recycle" hanging file and a separate "Shred" hanging file. Empty them when they each exceed two inches and celebrate your ongoing success!

Can I Do This in 20 Minutes?

That depends on how long it's been since you last cleared up your desk's paper pile. Usually twenty to thirty minutes once a week on Fridays will leave your desk and tasks organized for a smooth takeoff on Monday mornings. This catch-up on accumulated paperwork will take less time the more often you do it.

You can speed up the cleanup by standing until you get it done, avoiding all call or text interruptions, and even turning on music until you are finished. (Hang a "Do Not Disturb" sign or "Back in 20 Minutes" sign on your door. Set the timer on your phone for twenty minutes and begin!)

The Results? It will be the biggest relief to see a clean desktop and only a master to-do list in its place! You'll feel better and perform better the sooner you deal with that nagging paper pile. You can do it! Try it right now.

What Do I Do with the Master List?

Count the number of tasks on your master to-do list and divide it by five days. That's how many tasks you need to do each day to catch up in a week. If that's too much, divide it by ten and give yourself two weeks. If that's too much, cross off 10 percent of the items to make sure only your highest-priority actions remain on the list.

Your Instant Insights...

- When you start to get mentally fuzzy at work, take twenty minutes, clear off any paper piles on your desk, and write a master to-do list.

- Be time efficient by scheduling the top five to-do items from your master list on this week's calendar.

- Stay organized by turning all paper piles into a master list once a week. It's so freeing!

Organize Your File Drawers

File drawers are 'hidden gold' for organizing all your paperwork!

Organizing your files can sound as dreadful as going to the dentist ... unless you have a plan that shows you exactly where to start, how to move through files quickly, and how to get everything put back into its new location. It can be done, and here's the step-by-step plan.

The good news is we start with the oldest files first; that will help you reclaim file-drawer space for current projects. The best news is once your files are organized and old papers recycled, you'll make room for your current files. The top file drawer will hold your current work.

Start with Sticky-Note Prioritizing

Begin by reviewing the file drawers in your desk or right next to your desk. Because they are closest to you, these drawers should be the most organized. Put a sticky note with "Priority #1, #2, or #3" on each one to begin the organizing process. Here are some examples on how to do this:

#1 Drawer – The file drawer closest to you at desktop height is for "Current Work" and is worth "Gold"! No more excusing piles on the desktop with "keeping things handy." Once you commit to holding your current projects and work in this drawer and everything inside the drawer is listed on your calendar or master list, it won't be forgotten. The drawer contents will be changing as you complete work and move on to your next projects.

#2 Drawer – This should be labeled with the name of your next most-used work. Think in terms of a whole drawer by that topic, such as "Financials" if you are an accountant, "Major Initiatives" if you are an executive, or "Clients" if you are an entrepreneur.

#3 Drawer – This third priority drawer should contain your third priority topic, which you will label by that name, such as "Vendors" or "Past Clients." This drawer is more for filing and retrieval by category rather than current usage—important but not urgent.

Additional File Drawers – These separate file drawers should be numbered in priority of importance and frequency of use until all the files have sticky notes with numbers on them.

How Many Total File Drawers Do You Have?

Your files, piles, and boxes of papers have to fit into your total number of file drawers. If you have papers beyond those drawers or they are so stuffed that you can't put another thing into them, it's time for a big cleanout—which is the next step!

Don't Begin File Organizing without a Strategy!

As the leading online organizing coach, I keep my clients out of trouble and prevent them from making a mess of their office with file-drawer organizing by creating a strategy specific for their situation. My first tip is this: don't take anything out of a file drawer to sort unless you have a plan for where those specific files are going in the reorganization.

The Plan Is "Review and Release"

Begin sorting your oldest files first. This is likely the last number of your already prioritized sticky notes.

Take six to ten inches of those files from the back of the oldest file drawer and place them on your clear desktop with a recycle bin on the floor next to you.

Begin from the back of the stack and release what you don't need. Consolidate papers if they can go into another file, and recycle whatever you can. As you work, you will develop a rhythm to your sorting, and you will be creating new space. The goal is to retain only current files and have as few files as possible.

Be Decisive with File Sorting

The key to successfully getting through your files is to be decisive when you first look at the papers inside them. Ask these two questions:

1) Is this file part of my past, or my present and future? If it's part of your past, let it go to recycle and free up space.

2) Do I really want to see this paper again, or should I let it go now? If in doubt, throw it out.

Our slogan for sorting papers is "Use it or Lose it." Keep a file only if it serves your present and future work. Keep moving quickly through this review of your file drawers and fill the recycle bin with everything you can!

The Goal in Organizing Your File Drawers

All your papers should fit into your available file drawers. "Current Work" should be easily accessible and closest to your desk. Business or tax archival files could be the exception if you don't have room in your office and if they can be stored offsite or elsewhere.

How Much Time Will This Take?

A better question would be, "How much more efficient will I be if I know exactly where my papers are filed, and other people could find them organized and well labeled if I were not available?" My experience is that any file organizing will last you five to ten years of regular use.

It's usually best to do file reorganizing after work or on a weekend. One of my business clients inherited an office filing system that never worked for her and made her want to look for a new job. With our weekly coaching and accountability lessons, she reorganized fourteen file drawers in three weeks by spending an hour and a half after work each day and two to three hours on the weekend. When she finished the task, she had another job offer, but her boss gave her a raise so she stayed ... and enjoyed her streamlined setup that made her workday so much easier. It was a win-win for the time invested!

Conclusion

If you continually have paperwork on your desk or are stumbling over disorganized client or project files in meetings, scheduling an annual organizing swoop through your files will save your time and reputation, which increases your bottom line. It's worth it to reorganize file drawers to support your busy workday, whether you do it all at once or over time. Generally, your file system will last five to ten years once you thoroughly reorganize the contents.

Your Instant Insights...

- The key to file-drawer organizing is to neatly label and categorize files by drawer for the fastest retrieval.

- Begin the momentum to sort through file drawers by going through the drawer you use least to find new space.

- It's important to continually update your "Current Work" file drawer closest to you.

Catch Up on the Backlog

Feel the satisfaction of catching up one shelf, one box, one corner of your office at a time. Reduce the stress of things sitting around, measure your results in pounds recycled, and complete the job of going through everything in your office.

What's left to do in your office? Stand back right now from your work area and scan the desktop, bookshelves, and floor as if you are seeing everything for the first time. Does the area excite you with efficiency and say to your clients or visitors that you have it together?

Of course, you know that it would be best to continue if there are boxes on the floor, piles of files, binders lined up that you never touch, and a cluttered bulletin board. But how do you get motivated? Here is where the fun begins ...

How Do I Get Motivated to Finish Organizing?

"Make your organizing memorable and fun" is one of my organizing rules. I have lost thirty pounds of paper in a week by doing just that. All you need to do is set a date in the next three weeks, get a scale, and chart your progress of things you eliminate from your workspace.

My "paper diet" started when my husband's work limited what they would pay to move. It cost sixty cents to move a pound at the time. I wasn't going to get rid of my book collection, but I figured I had some files, binders, and favorite magazines I could cull through. So I set my goal of a thirty-pound "paper diet" in three weeks. It worked, and I set my goal higher every year.

The 30-Pound Paper Diet

The goal of the paper diet is to motivate you to finish going through all binders, cabinet items, flat surfaces, floor items, and remaining files to stay "clean and lean"! Decluttering your entire workspace is fun when you keep track of the weight of what you have removed.

Just today, a client of mine was so excited to report that she had recycled twenty-two pounds and shredded sixteen pounds in the past two weeks. That means Mary had "lost" almost forty pounds of needless paper in fourteen days! Mary went on to say, "I find I actually like to throw things out, besides gaining new space. I've been sorting through paper thirty minutes a night after work. With five drawers of papers finished that were over ten years old and eight boxes to go, I know I will finish in the next three weeks."

What Do I Include in the Backlog Catch-Up?

Catch-up on the backlog is usually done on a weekend or after work. It can involve moving boxes, cleaning shelves, shredding papers, and carrying out heavy bags. Or it could be as simple as taking a few things home and dusting your shelves. It all depends on what you tolerate in your space.

There are five areas to scrutinize in your workspace to complete the job of organizing and creating a workspace for maximum productivity. Soon you'll be free to fully engage yourself in your work.

1. Boxes Are Postponed Decisions

Boxes in a corner or under a desk are postponed decisions, and NOW is the time to go through and eliminate them! They need to be incorporated, discarded, or moved to storage IF they will have a near-future purpose to be used. There's never a better time to go through them, and it's certainly rewarding to deliver or recycle the entire contents of the box(es) until everything is off the floor.

2. Purge the Personal Items

Seriously, take these things home: silverware, shoes, jacket, gym bags, lunch supplies. You'd be surprised how often I find a perfectly good file drawer cluttered with food and personal items that haven't been touched in months ... nor will they ever be. Clean them out, and you'll have gained "golden" file space!

3. Every 3-Ring Binder Doesn't Need to Be Kept

Go through all your binders and scan or pitch them as most business products or procedures are now online. Rarely is there a need for more than a few binders, and those you keep are those you create as your own personal reference material.

Binders account for a huge amount of "weight loss" in your paper diet. Weigh bags of discarded papers, binders, and recycled papers, and feel and see the freedom letting go allows.

4. Books and Shelving Require Housekeeping

Make sure your books and shelving are clutter-free and appealing to work around. Books should stand vertically on your bookshelves with nothing lying sideways on top of them. On average, books weigh a pound per hardback and benefit you and other people only if they are read. Review the necessity of keeping them by dusting each one and donating those that are just there for prestige and not for use.

5. Magazines Should Be Circulated

Magazines are beneficial if you keep up on the reading because they provide current, deeper information than fast-paced Internet reading.

Even in your favorite collection, consider clipping one to two articles per magazine and then donating them to a hospital or school. That way you have prioritized and minimized your reading, and you have benefited someone else who can use them, too. Plus, you will have pounds of magazines to add to the paper diet and new, updated space for only current magazines.

Rule of Thumb for Magazines and Newspapers: New one in, old one out, even if you have to read it on the spot.

You can now feel confident in your ability to get things done, and other people will have that same confidence in you now that your work area is well organized.

Your Instant Insights...

- Feel the satisfaction of catching up by eliminating piles, bags, and boxes to stay focused on your work.

- Multiply your productivity by taking control over your space and what you allow   into it.

- Stay organized by regularly cleaning up excess items on Fridays for a fresh start on Mondays.

Organize Your Computer Files Consistently

Speed up retrieval by carefully labeling your documents.

Did you know cleaning up your computer files can save you time and embarrassment?

Yes, indeed. You might have worked hard on a document, saved it, attached what you thought was the right file to an e-mail, and poof! Out went the wrong one, much to your embarrassment.

Why? Because of inconsistent labeling, too many files with similar titles, and failing to clean up folder content as you go.

Organizing your computer files can save you time. It takes only a few more minutes of attention to detail each day. Clean out as you go.

Speed Up the Cleanup

Screen time on our computers, smart phones, and social media takes up a lot of our day. You may be losing valuable time by wandering around in a maze of digital clutter. The solution? Consistently put these seven tips into action.

1. Clean Up Your Main Computer Screen

Begin by organizing your computer desktop screen. Do a quick sort by placing essential items on the left side of the screen. You'll spot them when you open your computer each day. Place random "file or delete" documents on the right side. A simple initial sort like this will enable you to easily handle several of the items on the right side each time you log in. Soon your screen will be clutter-free!

This is important because as the leader in PC optimization Iolo Technologies, LLC, says, "As a general rule, the state of your desktop is a pretty good indicator of the overall organization of your computer." Start getting yours in tip-top shape today.

2. Simplify with Folders

Unending lists of documents in your computer are visual clutter! Create the "big picture" organization of your documents by creating category "folders" of the main activities you normally need as you work, such as:

- Clients
- Financials
- Meetings
- Personal
- Products
- Projects
- Reports
- Trainings

Keep the topics broad enough so that you have only about ten to twenty folders to scan down. Within these folders are your files.

3. Consolidate Files into Folders

In each folder you will put files related to the topic. When you put ten to twenty files on the same topic in one folder, it's much simpler to find things. If there are several categories within a topic, create a smaller folder with a right click on "New Folder."

Example: The folder "Personal" can have more folders in it, such as "Donations," "Family Reunion," "Finances," "Gift Ideas," "Health," "Parties," "People," and "Vacations."

Sure, you can use the search feature to find what you are looking for, but it's faster and more efficient to place ten to twenty files in one folder. Stop the mental confusion and brain drain by placing your single documents in a larger category folder.

4. Rename the "Odd Balls"

Oddballs are the leftovers, those documents that don't fit into any of your folders and dangle at the end of your folder list. Review them and find their category folder, or create a new folder for a group of them.

5. Be Consistent with First-Letter Labeling in Files

When you title documents, label them either alphabetically or by number, such as by year. When you create a file for documents of a similar topic, you are categorizing.

For example, you have a folder titled "Clients." Within that category, you will name every client by either their first or last name. Pick one way and use it consistently. Another category could be "Projects." Name these files by project name, type of project, or due date. For a final document, you can even CAPITALIZE the title for easy visual retrieval.

Standardize your document titles so that your eye can glance down all the similar topics and easily find the file you need. Just like an actual sheet of paper in a pile, putting computer documents into folders simplifies the visual clutter facing you and makes the document easy to find.

6. Add a Dash to the Top 5 Work Projects

One way to keep priority work top-of-mind each day is to keep them at the top of your folder list. You can do that by putting a dash [—] in the front of the title. *Voil*à!

A title such as "—Training" places that folder at the top of your folders, instead of having to scroll down to the "T" titles every day while you are planning the company training in Maui, though that is certainly worth the effort!

When that project is finished, delete the dash, and it falls immediately back into its normal alphabetical location.

7. Get Your Zzzzz's out of the Way!

When working on revisions of a document, you'll want to keep the newest document at the top of the list. A quick trick is to put a "z" in front of the older file(s), which moves it to the bottom of the document list. You'll have the security of knowing it's still there to refer to, but also the pleasure of confidently deleting all the "Zzzzz's" when a project is finished!

Your work can be so much more efficient when you successfully keep your computer files organized and up-to-date. You'll find anything in seconds, which is especially helpful for business meetings, client requests, and projects!

What happens if you don't successfully organize your computer files? You'll have a digital mess on your hands—that's worse than a messy workspace. The frustration will be so much greater if you can't find something you carefully and painstakingly wrote three days ago. No more!

The Result

You'll feel in control every time you open your computer and get to work from now on! You'll feel calmer and think more clearly when your computer documents are dependably organized.

Your Instant Insights...

- Digital document clutter can be cumbersome, but once you systematize it, you'll be set free to work with speed.

- Strategically labeled folders of your big-picture work categories will be the foundation of easily retrieving your documents.

- Stay organized and efficient by cleaning up your computer desktop regularly and thinking twice about your document titles before you close down your work.

Handle Your E-mail More Efficiently

Control your in-box before it controls you!

Do you feel overwhelmed by e-mail? Then it's time to take charge before it becomes "e-mail clutter!" Why? Because too many e-mails in your in-box are the beginning of a complicated life. Clean up your in-box after a block of work time and leave each day relaxed, knowing your e-mail is under control.

1. Read and Respond

Decide what to do the FIRST time you open an e-mail. Answer it right then, or it will double the time it takes to respond. You can take a break to catch up on e-mail after a focused block of time on a work project.

If you decide what to do the first time you read an e-mail, it will likely cut your work in half. It's like coming home and tossing your jacket on a chair. Later you have to go back, pick it up, and then put it away. Instead of a smooth, single step—walking in and hanging up your jacket right away—you've just doubled your work. Cut your work in half by handling your e-mails as soon as you open them … and hang up your jacket!

If an e-mail requires careful attention and more time to respond than you have right at the moment, keep it in your in-box and mark it as unread. Before lunch or leaving for the day, make sure you respond to all of those e-mails, even if your response is, "I'll get back to you in the morning on that." People appreciate being responded to the same day.

2. Clear It Out

Once you've read and responded, move it out of your in-box with "Delete" or "Archive." In "Archive" it's still there; you can search for it by keyword. If you're not ready to delete it and it's useful after a relatively short time, drag it into a folder you set up called "Temporary-This Month." Then review the e-mails in that folder on the last day of the month, highlight them all, and enjoy the thrill of hitting the delete button!

3. Strategize Your Signature

Review your email signature to include a compelling tag line that offers the reader further knowledge of your business and/or invites engagement by something you offer. It's perpetual marketing potential on every email you write.

4. Tame Your "Reading" File

Separate out the good blogs and newsletters that pass your way, and put them into this file. Read them midafternoon or at the end of the day. Delete "Reading" file contents weekly.

5. Create No More Than 6–10 Key E-mail Folders

Once you've responded to an e-mail, move it to a folder called "Responded," Holding," or "Archive." Move out e-mails older than three months to "Archive before (date)." Delete them if they're no longer needed.

6. Don't "Over File" with Too Many Specific Folders

Create no more than six to ten folders by program, action steps, or project. It's time-consuming to put them into any more folders than that. Rely on the search feature to pull up e-mails.

7. Create "Rules" in Outlook or "Filters" in Gmail

Creating these rules lets e-mail bypass your inbox and land in a folder for things you might want to review later. Create folders for general topics such as "Coupons" and "Newsletters," and redirect multiple e-mail lists there. Be selective and delete your subscription at the bottom of an e-mail of those you no longer read.

8. Set Times to Handle E-mail and Don't Let It Become Your To-Do List!

Twice in the morning and twice in the afternoon are adequate. Train yourself to stay away from e-mail for the first fifteen to thirty minutes of each day so that you can complete a top-priority task like a financial review or writing a proposal before you open e-mail.

9. Pare Down E-mail before You Close Your Computer

Fewer than twenty total e-mails in your in-box puts you in the driver's seat of your life.

Clean out2 newsletter and advertising e-mail weekly, at the end of each week. Read the key ones you've put in your "To Read" or "Promotions" folder, and then delete them all for a clean slate for the next week.

10. Do a Massive E-mail Backlog Cleanup

Settle in with a timer for twenty minutes or while listening to a podcast or webinar and go through your e-mail in-box from the oldest page to the newest with these steps:

- Highlight "All" on the last e-mail page (display 100).
- "Unclick" up to five of those you want to keep on that page.
- Hit "Trash Can" and delete the rest.
- Then highlight "ALL" of the few that are left.
- Click "Archive" down arrow.

Poof! You just got rid of 100 e-mails on that page!

Go to the next page and repeat the "Highlight All" and "unclick" keepers until you've gone through your whole in-box. You'll be so glad to have less than one screen of e-mails in your in-box.

What Are the Costs and Benefits of E-mail Control?

The cost is too much time spent wandering around a full in-box—rabbit trails, unproductive searches for important files, and valuable time lost on screen time.

The in-box control benefits are the time saved on e-mail, the ability to put your hands quickly on things, and the relief of knowing priorities are dealt with and extraneous inputs are being weeded out.

Your Instant Insights...

- Set a goal to cut your e-mail in half each week, and start now to get control.

- Pick a weekly day for in-box cleanup of reading material and to fine-tune anything you missed earlier.

- Stay organized by being intentional about controlling your e-mail instead of it controlling you.

Spruce Up Your Digital Presence

Everything online is a reflection of you!

Have you ever had someone look at your business card or show up on a virtual meeting platform and say, "Is this really you?!"

If so, that's a red flag that your digital presence—the title you have next to your name on everything you send out, your avatar photo on all your social media, and how you show up every day—needs a once-over housecleaning. Do you look like one and the same person, or are you in need of a digital update?

5 Ways to Spruce Up Your Digital Presence

An often quoted business principle says, "People do business with people they know, like, and trust." In today's online world, you instantly create that online "knowing, liking, and trusting" in the different ways you present yourself. People search you out online before they seek you out in person.

If they find you online first and like what they see, they carry this impression over into your first virtual or face-to-face meeting. You have to be as congruent online as possible.

1. Your Online Presence Should Be Consistent with Who You Are and What You Do

Think about it: If you met a financial planner in person for the first time, wouldn't you expect him or her to look professional and to convey they are trustworthy, knowledgeable, and friendly? Of course. Likewise, you want someone checking you out online to see you as someone who could handle their money well as well as someone they could get along with.

On the other hand, someone in the health and wellness industry would lower their credibility if they wrote you an e-mail at 2:00 a.m. because we all know sleep is essential to good health. Better yet, they could build their credibility by posting social media posts about their workouts and marathon runs. You'd trust that they live what they preach and would be more likely to interview them to get in shape.

To be consistent about what you put online, ask yourself if you are attracting the business you want by what you are posting.

2. Look Like Yourself Online

When someone asks, "Is this really you?" you know it's time to look at every photo you have online and change them immediately!

Personally, I take note of the avatar photos of new clients I am going to coach to get a feel for who they are. Recently I noticed the e-mail avatar of a new client, and when she showed up virtually at our scheduled time, I thought someone else was calling me at the wrong time. Her avatar showed a smiling, perky brunette with a stylish haircut, yet the lady who showed up virtually had long blonde hair that was less than polished for a first business meeting. She explained that the photo was old and she didn't have time to change it, but it gave the wrong first impression and hurt her credibility.

When you want to improve your business bottom line, changing your photo is a detail that may be low on your to-do list, but it should be the one you do immediately. Check your online photos ASAP.

3. Market Your Position Consistently

Likewise, your titles describing who you say you are and what you say you do should be consistent.

At a networking meeting you wouldn't hand out a business card and say, "Ignore the part about my dog-sitting business, but you can reach me at that cell phone number at city hall every day!"

Sure, you may have a sideline business (which most people do these days), but make sure your business cards and e-mails correctly reflect the business you are promoting. Use separate materials for your side work until it becomes your main work.

4. Coordinate Your Digital Messaging

Your website, LinkedIn, and social media branding beg for the real you to come through. Banner headings, consistent color and font choices, as well as an overall tone reflecting either a contemporary or traditional business style should be a cohesive unit. Just like a Target logo can be spotted anywhere, your business name, logo, or photo should be a designed marketing unit reflecting you, especially if you are an entrepreneur and need that professional-looking boost.

One of the first things I look at with an entrepreneur is the branding of their website. Honing in on key elements brings up questions, such as the following:

- Is your website banner current and consistent with what you represent?

- Do the color choices and fonts evoke a positive response from the market you want to attract?

- Is there an appealing entry-level opt-in connection or free call with you?

As a business productivity coach, I find strategic branding and consistency are key to building an online presence that magnifies their business so that they are ready to market fully. You rarely have a second chance online to create a first impression.

5. Live Your Values Online

You are a spokesperson for yourself and your business. If you write positive blogs and social media posts, people will probably keep reading what you write and follow you. If you go off on rants every couple weeks, you could be losing credibility with the people who watch you and your business.

I experienced this when my business team advised me to get a summer intern to help with social media expansion. We did our due diligence to find a hip young gal before settling on and approving a candidate. However, after a couple weeks, my social media linked back to hers, which showed photos of her in situations that were inconsistent with my business values.

We had a talk about our company's values and discussed her choice to take those particular photos down or step aside from her internship. She took some photos down, but soon after stepped out of the internship. A lesson learned: you and your business staff can express individuality, but not when it hurts the overall business exposure.

In other words, don't work for one company and brag about the competition. It's like working for Apple and talking about your PC that needs repair.

Your Instant Insights...

- Do an online search of your avatars on all social media platforms and see if what shows up is consistent messaging with you and your brand.

- Check out your e-mail signature and do your name search to see that they are building your digital presence in a positive way.

- Stay organized in the digital arena by updating any inconsistencies online as soon as you spot them.

Create a Dependable Planning Hub

"Keep what is working and change what is not."

The number-one problem I see as a business productivity coach is *not* having too much to do. It's not even too little time in which to do it. The main problem I've discovered is fragmentation— being pulled in many directions at once while trying to concentrate on the task at hand. Finding a solution to fragmentation so that you can stay focused is the biggest productivity issue you'll face in a day.

With at least 200–500 inputs a day, we have to make decisions on where to focus next while keeping an eye on what we need to do. Meanwhile, our minds work overtime, trying to remember everything we have to do, want to do, and should do. No wonder we are overwhelmed before we even begin!

What's the solution? Create a dependable planning hub you can count on to capture all the projects, to-do's, meeting information, and details you need to effectively focus and finish your work.

What Do You Do Currently?

Think about what you do during the day and—even broader—on what days of the week. Most of us would claim that no two days are alike. Although that's true, you do have a rhythm and pattern to what you do first, second, and third in a day.

With your workplace now organized, it's time to pull your work together in a planning hub with dependable systems to keep you focused and on track. These are your anchor systems for keeping up a productive rhythm.

3 Systems in a Planning Hub

A planning hub is the place with all your "go-to" systems, the systems you check first thing each morning and continuously throughout the day to keep you on task. I look for three key elements with every new business client:

1. A time-management system for calendaring the day's work and events

2. A task system for planning to-dos, projects, and client meetings, whether it be on Outlook, Gmail, or your favorite apps.

3. A financial system and regular review system to keep your financials in order, especially if you are the business owner or a sole proprietor.

Your planning hub can show up on your computer, or it can be posted on a board in front of you or written on a paper planner. It tells you priorities, projects, clients, and the to-do List for the day. Being able to pull together your many activities in one spot gives you control of your time and tasks.

A To-Do List – This is a list of tasks to accomplish in one day to achieve your longer-range goals. Plan a regular time to write up the list in high-, medium-, and low-priority order or with categories like calls, e-mails, customers.

A Master List – This is the list of all the projects that will need more than one day to complete. Write down things that cross your mind on your calendar and include it in your planning every week.

A planning hub is your personal assistant. You take everything on your mind and input it into a time and task plan for the day, week, and month. This is your personal business center, the place where you can see and plan what needs to be done in the time frame available.

When you miss deadlines, feel stuck in a rut, or find sticky notes all over your desk, take time to improve one aspect of your planning system. My motto is, "If you can't fit it all in your daily system, you can't live it in one day." That's the value of preplanning: you map out your time and task priorities ahead of time and learn what works best for you.

Busy—but Not Productive

One law firm called me in to train their attorneys— particularly one of them. Based on his overflowing piles of paperwork, disorganized work ethic, and lack of productivity, they felt he was a hazard to their firm. After meeting with all twelve in the firm, this lawyer came to a startling realization.

After we cleared up his many piles of paper and hung all his pictures, there was nothing left for him to view but his online planning system. His realization? "I thought I was so busy, but now I see I only spent 40 percent of my day actually working. I had no idea I was underperforming."

On the other hand, an insurance agent had hired and fired four people to handle his front office. He was blaming them for not building his business. In his case, once we cleared up all the papers in his office by assigning them to a date and time, he realized he had ten full days of his own work to do to get caught up! Suddenly the real problem became clear—and it wasn't the people in the front office.

Both gentlemen had clouded work perceptions until we took a look at their productivity and income. While one needed to get more work done, the other needed to focus on marketing in order to have more work to do.

They are now in a position to grow their businesses. Their time and task lists changed dramatically based on these new insights. When I went back to train new people at the law firm a year later, I was happy to see that they were so much more polished, professional, and focused on their productivity.

You're Not Getting Forgetful—You Just Need to Write It Down

This is key because studies have shown we can hold only seven items in our short-term memory. Add more, and we forget something until we put our head on the pillow at night. Forgetfulness may not mean we're getting old; we literally have too much on our minds!

So stop and write down the things you don't finish or attend to. They need to be integrated into your already working systems—on your calendar, to-do list, or master list. Otherwise, something valuable may slip through the cracks until it's too late in the day, week, month, or year to accomplish them.

3 Key Productivity Questions

Decide if your systems are supporting you with these three assessment questions:

1. Am I getting my priorities (my work, e-mails, contacts) finished on time and in the time I planned?

2. What do I always get done (expense reports, same-day e-mail responses, phone call returns)?

3. What is not getting done (long-range projects, proposal writing, budgeting)?

Be purposeful about the time tools you use, and jot down your plans at the end of the day for tomorrow or first thing in the morning. Taking all the important information off your mind enables you to prioritize or delete items more easily. When written out, your ideas and thoughts begin to take shape and become plans and projects in time frames. Your productivity will increase when you start with a well-planned day.

Your Instant Insights...

- Your planning tools you use every day are the foundation of your productivity and keep you focused.

- Save fifteen minutes of morning indecision by creating a time plan for the next day before leaving work.

- Stay organized with this principle: keep what is working; change what is not.

Work Smarter for a Productivity Edge!

The difference between average and excellence is 15 minutes.

Your productivity edge is the advantage you gain over your personal workload and past performance that makes you more successful by using these skills on a consistent basis.

These consciously chosen skills become habits that you know will bring you your best results every day. And if you skip them, your day is less than stellar and your work becomes mediocre.

What one productive habit can you think of right now that gives you the feeling that you're on top of things at work?

Every successful person tweaks their habits to acquire more productivity-edge skills and drops old habits that hold them back. This is the essence of time management—managing yourself and your habits, not time, in regards to the time available. Better skills equal better results.

The Difference between Average and Excellence Is 15 Minutes

Did you know that if you can invest just fifteen minutes a day into your top priority, you will reap sixty-five hours of success at the end of the year on that project?

15 Minutes x 5 Days = 1.25 Hours a Week or 5.4 Hours a Month or 65 Hours a Year!

Likewise, if you lose fifteen minutes a day, you will have lost over an hour weekly and 65 Hours a year of valuable time!

What Will You Gain—or Lose—This Year?

- How could fifteen minutes make a difference? Working smarter means looking for those fifteen minutes to bring your work from average to excellence by doing the following:

- Carefully proofread a proposal or important e-mail before sending it off, fixing mistakes, and setting the right tone.

- Confirm a meeting agenda and its attendees a day ahead, saving everyone's time and creating a reputation as someone who begins and ends meetings promptly.

- Review tomorrow the night before, writing down your top three priorities so that in the morning you can get right to work.

- Plan 15 minutes at the end of each day to bring closure to open ended items like emails and cleaning up your workspace.

- Get to sleep fifteen minutes earlier so that you can think better the next day and stay healthier long term.

People performing with excellence seek out those fifteen-minute advantages to spend on their priorities.

Practice the Half-Hour Habit "What 1 Thing ..."

Another skill to acquire is practicing the "half-hour habit." On the hour and half hour, ask yourself, "What one thing do I want to accomplish in the next half hour?"

This will give you sixteen focused and completed tasks if you work an eight-hour day. When you get lost in a muddle of mixed priorities and interruptions, it will quickly get you back on track. Train yourself to accurately guess the time, and on the hour and half hour, ask yourself that powerful but simple question, "What one thing do I want to accomplish in the *next* half hour?" And do it!

Do a Time Inventory for One Week

Did you know you are predictable? Indeed, even if you do something different every day.

One of the most powerful productivity tools I use with every new client is a time inventory of what they do every hour for one week using my famous 168 Hour Time Tracker. Once they see where their time is going and what they are not getting done, we make strategic adjustments to intentionally accomplish and improve their overall lifestyle.

For instance, one financial planner client was coming in at 9:00 a.m. and staying until 7:00 and 8:00 p.m. Why? As we explored the issue, it turned out she didn't like going home to her mother-in-law. Solution? We brainstormed where she could go at five thirty, like to tennis, shopping, or dinner with a friend, which would still allow her to get home later. It worked and she's much happier and more productive.

Work Smarter by Controlling Your Power Hours

Everyone has a "power hour" where they can buckle down and produce amazing results in a short period of time. Controlling your power hours for strategic activities is your secret to getting the most out of your day. You need three in a day.

Morning Power Hour: The early bird gets the worm if you are a morning person but loses it without a strategy. Plan productive priority projects for the week on Sunday night, and mark them as appointments. Get up earlier, like at 5:00 or 6:00 a.m., to keep those appointments with yourself.

Noon Power Hour: Noon is a great power hour to meet with clients, coworkers, or friends. Schedule this "people power hour" time for two lunches per week on a weekly basis, such as on Tuesdays and Thursdays.

Afternoon Power Hour: The "wrap-up power hour" is the time to bring closure for the day's work. The hour before you finish for the day, close down e-mail, finish the project at an appropriate stopping point, make final phone calls, and write a list of priorities you will pick up with tomorrow morning.

Strategically utilize the rhythm to your day to always put your best work, your people time, and your closure hour at the same time each day. You'll realize, "If I don't do this project at this time, I'll never get back to it." So you'll schedule it and do it. It's freeing, and the results will be amazing!

Work Smarter with a Weekly Work Rhythm

A higher-level step up is to be smart about the week. It's not the best use of time to plan your best work first thing Monday morning. Why? Because that's the heaviest day for incoming phone calls and team meetings. Instead, plan productive time on Tuesday, Wednesday, or Thursday mornings while meetings get scheduled in the afternoons.

List all the activities you have to do for your work and personal life. Track when these are getting done (or not done).

You'll discover that you always have time for what you do first! Switch up the order of your tasks and accomplish the priorities you're not getting done. You not only get those things off your mind, you also get them off your to-do list.

Your Instant Insights...

- The difference between average and excellent is only fifteen minutes a day to give you a productivity edge.

- You always have time for what you do first. Surprise yourself and move something from the bottom of the list to the top!

- Earn more time in your life by doing a time inventory for one week, get coached, and put the productivity edge to work in your life to produce your best work every day. I'm here for you!

Folders (PNG)

- Incidents
- Safety Mtg Attendance
- Audits
- Data Hub
- Concur
- SC Calls (PNG)
- Duke Safety Calls
- Field Visits
- Safety mailbox
- Head count
- mileage

About the Author

Marcia Ramsland is well known as the "Organizing Pro," a Business Productivity Expert, a national speaker, and Best Selling author of the *Simplify Your Life: Get Organized and Stay that Way* book series, which has sold over 100,000 copies. Marcia is a nationally recognized media guest, appearing in *Woman's Day*, *Real Simple*, Martha Stewart radio, and *The Wall Street Journal*.

Marcia's expertise includes one-on-one virtual coaching, business consulting, and speaking. Marcia has organized hundreds of client offices and businesses from corporate executive suites and office cubicles to solo entrepreneurs working from home offices. Thousands of audience participants from New York to California agree with her belief that anyone can become more organized and productive—even YOU!

Marcia's consistent mission for three decades continues to be *"Coaching Busy People to Make Every Day Count!"*

All her resources, coaching, and online classes are available on her website at www.organziingpro.com.

Folders (Home)

- Financial
  a) Banking
  b) Credit Cards
  c) Edward Jones
  d) PNG
  e) Retirement
  f) Bills
  g) Randolph Bank
  h) Carolina Bank
  i) Charles Schwab

- Health Records
  a) Diane
  b) Ronald
  c) Pets

- Subscriptions
- Fly Lady
- Family Records
- Diet Tips
- Dad's Stuff
- Mortgage (Home)
- Steve Pace
- PNG
- Photos

- Home

- Legal
- Valuables

- Insurance
  a) Auto
  b) Home
  c) Life
  d) Hagerty
  e) Accidental

- Warranties
- Personal: a) Diane b) Ronald
- Utilities (Phone, Cable, Davidson Consumer Cellular
- MSP
- Vehicles
- Comics
- Clayco
- Dell

Connect with the Author

Website:
Website: www.OrganizingPro.com

E-mail:
marcia@organizingpro.com

Social media:
Facebook:
https://www.facebook.com/
MarciaRamslandYourOrganizingPro

LinkedIn:
https://www.linkedin.com/in/marciaramsland

Twitter: @marciaramsland1

Pinterest:
https://www.pinterest.com/marciaramsland
You Tube: youtube.com/marciaramsland

Address:
16369 Alipaz Ct., Suite 102
San Diego, CA 92127

Other Books by this Author

Simplify Your Life: Get Organized and Stay That Way!

Simplify Your Time: Stop Running and Start Living!

Simplify Your Space: Create Order and Reduce Stress!

Simplify Your Holiday Season: Turn Seasonal Stress into Holiday Success!

All books available
at www.OrganizingPro.com

About Crescendo Publishing

Crescendo Publishing is a boutique-style, concierge VIP publishing company assisting entrepreneurs with writing, publishing, and promoting their books for the purposes of lead-generation and achieving global platform growth, then monetizing it for even more income opportunities.

Check out some of our latest best-selling AuthorPreneurs at http://CrescendoPublishing.com/new-authors/.

About the Instant Insights™ Book Series

The *Instant Insights™ Book Series* is a fact-only, short-read, book series written by EXPERTS in very specialized categories. These high-value, high-quality books can be produced in ONLY 6-8 weeks, from concept to launch, in BOTH PRINT & eBOOK Formats!

This book series is FOR YOU if:

- You are an expert in your niche or area of specialty

- You want to write a book to position yourself as an expert

- You want YOUR OWN book – NOT a chapter in someone else's book

- You want to have a book to give to people when you're speaking at events or simply networking

- You want to have it available quickly

- You don't have the time to invest in writing a 200-page full book

- You don't have a ton of money to invest in the production of a full book – editing, cover design, interior layout, best-seller promotion

- You don't have a ton of time to invest in finding quality contractors for the production of your book – editing, cover design, interior layout, best-seller promotion

For more information on how you can become
an *Instant Insights™* author,
visit **www.InstantInsightsBooks.com**

More Books in the
Instant Insight™ Series

A Time Management System for Creative Entrepreneurs
Mireille Riordan, Ph.D.

Branding and Website Essentials for Entrepreneurs
Melody Hunter

How to Create & Build a Successful Beauty Business
Erica Akao

Organizing Your Workspace for a Productivity Boost
Marcia Ramsland

How to Be a Happy & Prosperous CEO
Jodi Young

Taking Your Business from Startup to Thrive in 45 Days
Jodi Mosters

7 Strategies for Raising Calm, Inspired, & Successful Children
Dr. Eileen Fogel Colombise, Ph.D.

Creating a Solid, Lasting Connection with Your Kids
Dr. Vicki Panaccione

12 Leadership Powers for Successful Women
Sylvia Becker-Hill

MOTIVATION! Your Master Key to Success & Riches
Parviz Firouzgar

PERFORMANCE POWER: Clarity, Confidence & Joy
Molly Mahoney

Practical Natural Healing Tips for Vibrant Living
Leon Kuoisik

Crescendo
CrescendoPublishing.com

56137428R00055

Made in the USA
Lexington, KY
13 October 2016